NYLON TRACKSUIT

Wayne Jackman.

Reading Consultant:
Diana Bentley
University of Reading

Commissioned photographs:
Chris Fairclough

Our clothes

Denim Jeans
Leather Shoes
Nylon Tracksuit
Plastic Raincoat
Woolly Hat

Editor: Janet De Saulles

First published in 1990 by
Wayland (Publishers) Ltd
61 Western Road, Hove
East Sussex, BN3 1JD, England

© Copyright 1990 Wayland (Publishers) Ltd

British Library Cataloguing in Publication Data
Jackman, Wayne
  Nylon tracksuit.
  1. Fabrics
  I. Title II. Fairclough, Chris III. Series
  677'.02864

HARDBACK ISBN 1–85210–885–1

PAPERBACK ISBN 0–7502–0567–9

Phototypeset by Rachel Gibbs, Wayland
Printed and bound by Casterman S.A., Belgium

Contents

Nylon is a material 4

Nylon is good for making tracksuits 6

Nylon and the silkworm 8

The nylon thread is made 10

The yarn is made into fabric 12

The factory 14

The final stages 16

What else is nylon used for? 18

Things to do 20

Glossary 22

Books to read 23

Index 24

All the words that appear in **bold** are explained in the glossary on page 22.

Above These children like wearing tracksuits.

Nylon is a material

Our clothes can be made from many different materials or fabrics. Some of these are **natural**, such as wool, cotton or silk. Others, such as nylon or acrylic, are **synthetic**. Synthetic fabrics are made by using **chemicals**. Nylon is one of the most useful of these synthetic fabrics.

Right Many tracksuits are made from nylon or from a mixture of nylon and other materials.

4

Today, there are so many different types of synthetic fabrics that it can be difficult to remember all the different names. Often we say that things are made of nylon even when really they are made from a mixture of materials.

Above *Tracksuits are good for running in.*

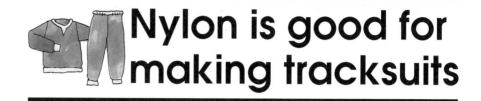
Below The girls in this Dutch softball team are wearing tracksuits.

People often wear nylon tracksuits when they play sports because nylon is so light and hard-wearing. Also, it does not tear easily when we are rough with it! It is very stretchy which makes it comfortable to wear, and useful when we need to jump and run. Nylon has many uses, but is especially good for playing sports as it is not damaged at all if we get hot or sweaty.

Imagine how dirty your tracksuit could get if you played in a muddy field in winter. Luckily, dirt does not stick easily to nylon, and because nylon always keeps its shape it can be washed again and again. It dries very quickly too, and usually does not even need to be ironed!

Above *Mud and other dirt can easily be washed off nylon.*

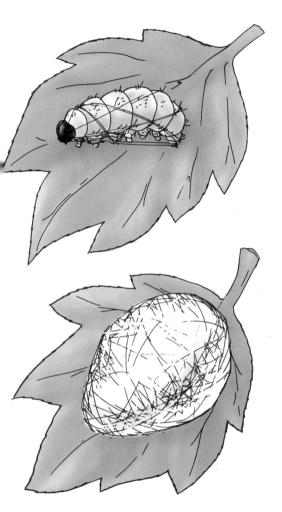

Nylon and the silkworm

Scientists discovered how to make synthetic fibres like nylon by watching the **silkworm**. A silkworm pushes out a liquid through tiny holes in its body. This liquid cools down in the air and hardens into a thread of silk. The scientists copied this idea by using chemicals to make nylon.

Above and **Right**
Silkworms spinning silk.

Some synthetic fibres, such as rayon, are made using natural or vegetable products such as **wood-pulp** or waste cotton. Nylon is different. It is made from chemicals found in air, coal, water, oil, natural gas and even oats and rice.

water

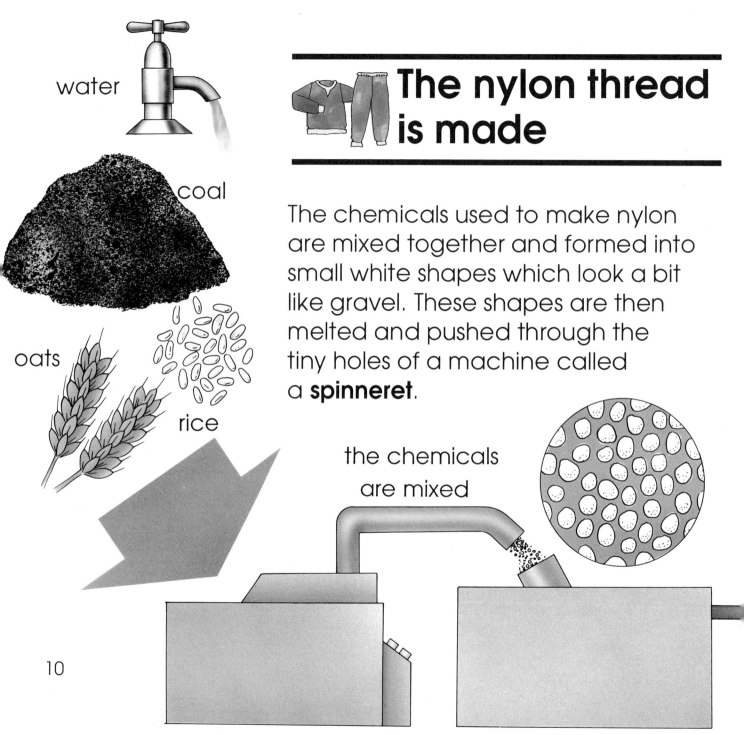

coal

oats

rice

The nylon thread is made

The chemicals used to make nylon are mixed together and formed into small white shapes which look a bit like gravel. These shapes are then melted and pushed through the tiny holes of a machine called a **spinneret**.

the chemicals are mixed

The liquid shoots out just like water from a shower. Cold air is blown over the jets of warm liquid. This makes the liquid become hard. Each jet of liquid has now become a piece of nylon thread. The threads are then stretched on rollers to become nylon yarn.

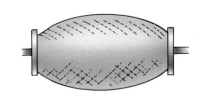

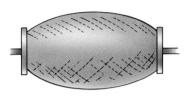

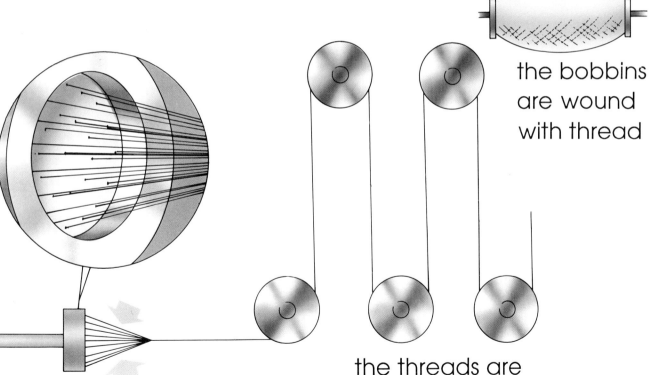

the bobbins are wound with thread

the threads are stretched on rollers

e jets of liquid are dried

The yarn is made into fabric

Nylon yarn can be **woven** into fabric. A **loom** is used to thread the strands in and out of each other. Sometimes the yarn is cut into short pieces which are **spun** to make the nylon thicker. The nylon can then be knitted into fabric. This kind of nylon is best for tracksuits.

spinning

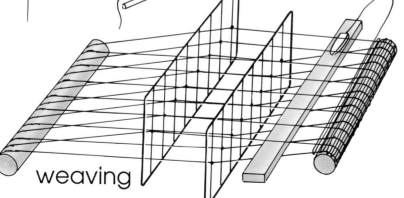

weaving

woven fabric

12

Nylon can be **dyed** many different colours. It keeps its colour well and does not fade. This means that tracksuits can be dyed to suit a particular team's colours. They are fun for everyday wear too!

Below *Tracksuits are useful for everyday wear.*

The factory

The nylon fabric is now delivered to the sportswear factory. Here it is cut and sewn into clothing. All sorts of sportswear can be made from nylon. As well as making tracksuits, a factory might make swimming costumes, football shirts and cycling shorts. The designer plans what the tracksuit will look like and the **patterns** are then made up.

Right Can you see the patterns on top of the piece of material?

Modern factories produce thousands of identical clothes. In many factories automatic machines do most of the work. Computers and robots cut out the fabric and sew the pieces together. Other machines are still worked by people in order to add the zips, elasticated waistbands and decorative stripes.

15

Above This child is trying on his new tracksuit.

Right The tracksuits are packed and sent to the shops.

 # The final stages

Once the nylon tracksuit has been sewn together it can be given a final treatment called heat-setting. It is held in shape and heated. Because nylon is a sort of plastic, this heat is really melting it into shape. Afterwards, the tracksuit will keep its shape and will not shrink.

Left *Tracksuits are comfortable to wear for all types of sport.*

The tracksuits are then packed and delivered to the shops. These can be big department stores or small specialized sports shops. Sportswear often comes from countries such as Hong Kong or Singapore. If you ever visit a sports shop have a look at some tracksuits – the labels should tell you where they were made.

What else is nylon used for?

There are hundreds of types of nylon. Each one has a slightly different use. Qiana nylon is very smooth and fine and is often used to make dresses.

Above *Nylon can be made into skipping ropes.*

Right *These fishing rods have lines made from nylon.*

Left *Tents made of nylon are both light and strong.*

Nylon is not only used to make clothes. It is also used for things such as car tyres, fishing lines, ropes, tents, sails, parachutes, carpets and even **artificial** grass!

One more reason why nylon is useful is because it can be mixed with other fibres such as wool, cotton and silk. Clothes made from these mixtures are light and strong as well as warm and soft. We get the best of both worlds.

Above *Nylon is difficult to crease.*

Things to do

1 Try to find a nylon shirt. Soak it in a sink full of clean water. Now hang it up on a hanger – how long do you think it will take to dry? Probably no more than an hour or two.

2 If you have a nylon tracksuit, try stretching it and crumpling it up into a ball. What do you notice when you let go? It will spring back into shape and leave no creases.

3 Examine the labels in your clothes. Can you find any that say they are made of nylon? You might find one that says it is a nylon **blend**. Perhaps the labels mention other synthetic

Left *Nylon is easy to wash and dries quickly.*

Below *See what your clothes are made from by examining their labels.*

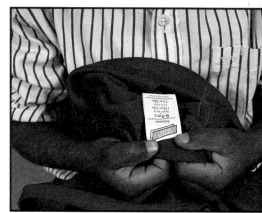

fibres. Here is a list of some to look out for: nylon, polyester, rayon, acetate, acrylic, lycra, spandex, terylene, crimplene, viscose. How many of each have you found?

Glossary

Artificial Something which is not found in nature.

Blend When two or more things have been mixed up together.

Chemicals Substances which are used in chemistry. Bleach is a well-known chemical.

Dyed Coloured.

Loom Machine for weaving fabric.

Natural Something found in nature.

Patterns The drawings which show what shape the tracksuit should be.

Silkworm The larva of the Chinese moth.

Spinneret A machine which has lots of small holes – it is rather like the head of a shower.

Spun Nylon which has been twisted into a long thread.

Synthetic Something which humans have made and is not found in nature.

Wood-pulp Wood which has been broken down into a soggy mass.

Woven When the nylon threads are passed in and out of each other to make material.

Books to read

Children's Clothes by Miriam Moss (Wayland, 1988)

How Clothes are Made by Sue Crawford (Wayland, 1987)

How It's Made: Clothing and Footwear by Donald Clarke (Marshall Cavendish, 1978)

Textiles by Stella Robinson (Wayland, 1983)

Index

Blend 20
Bobbins 11

Chemicals 4, 8, 9, 10
Christie, Linford 15
Christyokova, Galina 9

Designer 14
Dreschler, Heike 9
Dutch 6
Dyed 13

Fabrics 4, 5, 12, 15
Factory 14, 15
Fibres 8, 9, 21

Hong Kong 17

Joyner, Jackie 9

Knitted 12

Labels 17, 20, 21

Materials 4, 5, 14, 15
Mixtures 5, 15, 19

Natural 4

Patterns 14
Plastic 16

Scientists 8
Seams 15
Shops 16, 17
Silk 4, 8
Silkworm 8
Singapore 17
Spinning 12
Sports 7
Sportswear 14
Synthetic 4, 5, 8, 9, 20

Thread 8, 10, 11

Washing 7, 21
Wool 4

Acknowledgements

The author and Publisher would like to thank Hope Leisurewear Ltd, Bournemouth, and the Headteachers and staff of St Bernadette's School, Clapham Park, London, and of Middle Street School, Brighton, Sussex, for all their help in the production of this book.

They would also like to thank the following for allowing their photographs to be reproduced in this book: All Sport 9; Duncan Raban 15; Oxford Scientific Films 8; Topham Picture Library 6, 17. The illustrations on pages 8, 10, 11, 12 and 16 are by Janos Marffy.